GW01336947

Believe in Yourself

Change Your Mind and Change Your Life

Janice Johnson

authorHOUSE®

AuthorHouse™ UK Ltd.
500 Avebury Boulevard
Central Milton Keynes, MK9 2BE
www.authorhouse.co.uk
Phone: 08001974150

© 2009 Janice Johnson. All rights reserved.

No part of this book may be reproduced, stored in a retrieval system, or transmitted by any means without the written permission of the author.

First published by AuthorHouse 9/25/2009

ISBN: 978-1-4389-9072-9 (sc)

This book is printed on acid-free paper.

"I am just in awe of the exquisite, eloquent way that you express and tackle such difficult emotionally, life-changing issues, through such a high-powered wisdom, that to me seems utterly unique and yet so simply described in a common-sense way, that any person from whatever background or educational standard, couldn't help but derive pleasure and an immense optimism for life and for their future."

Alan T Brookes
Author and Publisher

*Change your mind
and
Change your life*

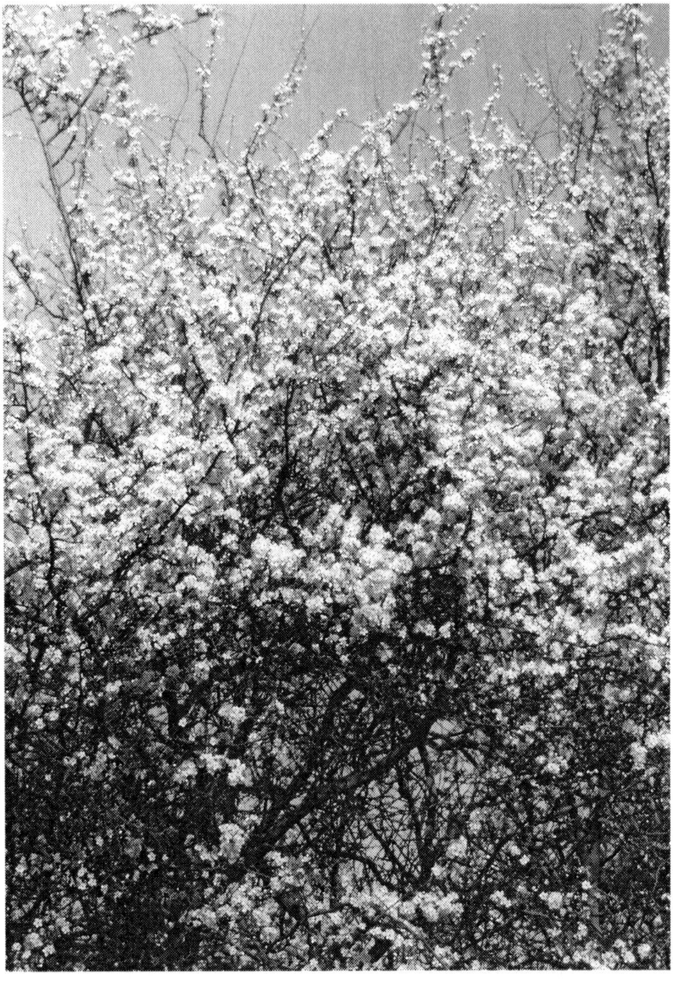

Dedicated to the Memory of

Mom, Dad and Audrey

X

ACKNOWLEDGEMENTS

I would like to thank my husband Peter,
my daughters, Nicola, Helen and Joanne and also
my son-in-law Nick, for their love and never ending
support.

This book also benefited from the following
contributions:

Glenys, my dear cousin, for proof-reading.
Sandra for her insight and faith.
Jon for his years of encouragement.

With much love and many thanks to you all.

I was so grateful that you all believed in me.

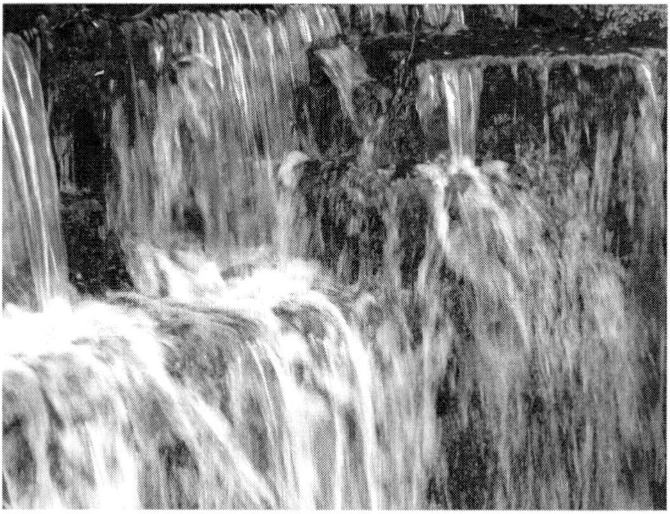

Contents

THE GOOD, THE BAD AND THE UGLY	1
LOOKING BACK	5
LOSS	11
UPS AND DOWN, DOWN, DOWNS	17
FAILURE	23
LOOK BEYOND THE PROBLEM	27
MAKING CHANGES	33
CONFIDENCE	37
DIVORCE	41
ANGER	45
CRITICISM	49
FORGIVENESS	55
BELIEFS	59
MAKE THE MOST OF LIFE	63
LOOKING TO THE FUTURE	67
CONCLUSION	71
CDs available by the same Author:	78
About the Author	81

We are shaped by our experiences, but we also shape our experiences.

THE GOOD, THE BAD AND THE UGLY

When will it end?
How will it stop?
Will death be the answer?
I hope not!

My head is exploding.

My body is wound up like a coiled spring.

When will I let go of the past?

Why am I hanging onto the humiliations and slights of the past?

At times there is so much anger inside me.

Isn't it time to forgive myself and others?

I would like the final season of my life to be peaceful and harmonious.

At the moment I am being eaten away with the injustices of the past.

I feel so alone.

I wrote all this a few years ago and it hurts me to read it. I am upset by my pain and the emotionally deep wounds.

Yes, I still bear the scars, and the remaining scabs will bleed if I knock them. There is still work to be done on myself.

In this book I have written openly about aspects of life and its emotions. My wish is that the truth in these pages will inspire and bring you hope.

I encourage you to make the journey towards gaining peace and contentment for yourself and to bring more happiness into your life.

*Remember the ugly duckling and
how he was transformed into a beautiful swan.
You too can cast off the ugliness of the past,
and see how beautiful you are.*

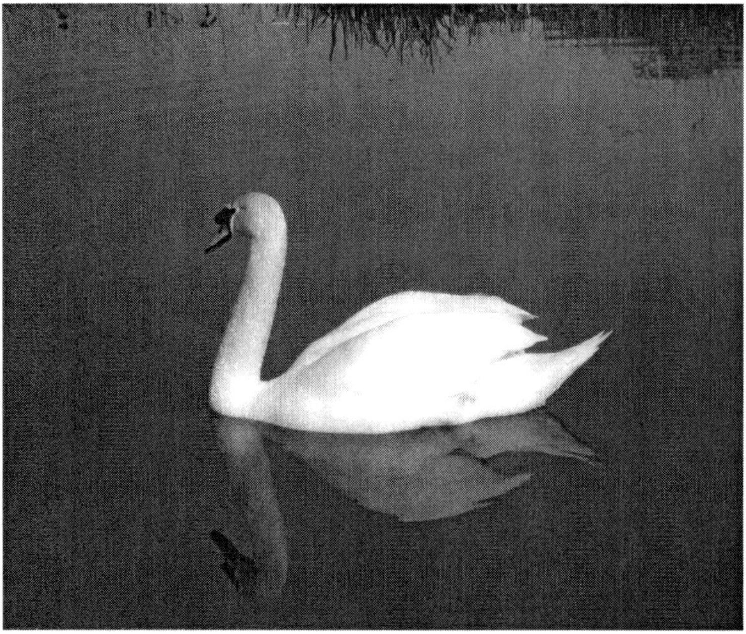

Maybe it's time to put past issues where they belong – firmly in the past.

LOOKING BACK

*As I walk
Through the avenues of life,
There is time to reflect,
And see the panorama of years past.*

Having a perfectionist for a father was difficult. I had a lot to live up to. But of course I never could.

Looking back I can see how the foundations of my character were being formed. These would influence me for a long time to come.

One of the high spots in my childhood was having a grandmother who loved me unconditionally.

Many seeds are sown in childhood but the good news is that as you become older and wiser you can sow your own seeds.

*Hello,
Who are you?
I do not know,
Do you?*

The journey of self discovery has been a long one. It is hard work and sometimes I felt it would have been easier to give in and stay the way I was. Inside I had become a negative person. Outside I put on a brave front. I felt like the swan – gliding serenely on the surface but paddling furiously underneath to keep up.

Do I blame anyone? No. Blame is the avoidance of responsibility.

As an adult there is so much to look back on with regret, blame, guilt, anger, resentment and so on. Okay, we have good memories too, but it tends to be the bad ones we focus on.

Naturally we do feel bad if we tell ourselves bad things.

Now each day I find there is always something to be thankful for. I try to adopt an attitude of gratitude. I say try because it is hard to do things right all the time.

Life is never perfect and neither are we.

Oh, the post mortems I have had!

"Why did I say that?" "Why didn't I do this or that?"

Blame – didn't do and should have. Guilt – did do and shouldn't have.

Did they do any good? No! It was just another way of beating myself up.

Of course, what does work is to say, "Well never mind, that was how I did it then, but next time I can handle things better." I can learn from the past because these negative experiences bring with them a positive lesson.

Yes I still look back over my shoulder at the past. It is hard weaning yourself off such habitual negative appraisals but I am now aware of what I am doing and take appropriate steps to deal with each incidence of backward vision.

So how can you let go of the negative past?

By acknowledging its existence.
By accepting it for what it was.
By remembering it doesn't determine who you become.
By forgiving yourself.
By forgiving others (not necessarily condoning their behaviour).
By letting go of the past negative reminders.
Affirm to yourself, "I accept and release the negative past and am prepared to move forward".

We have to accept that we cannot change the past.

What we can do is create the future by what we do in the present. Now when I look back I can see many good times as they are no longer overshadowed by the bad.

> *Memories are the threads*
> *That make up the cloth of life.*

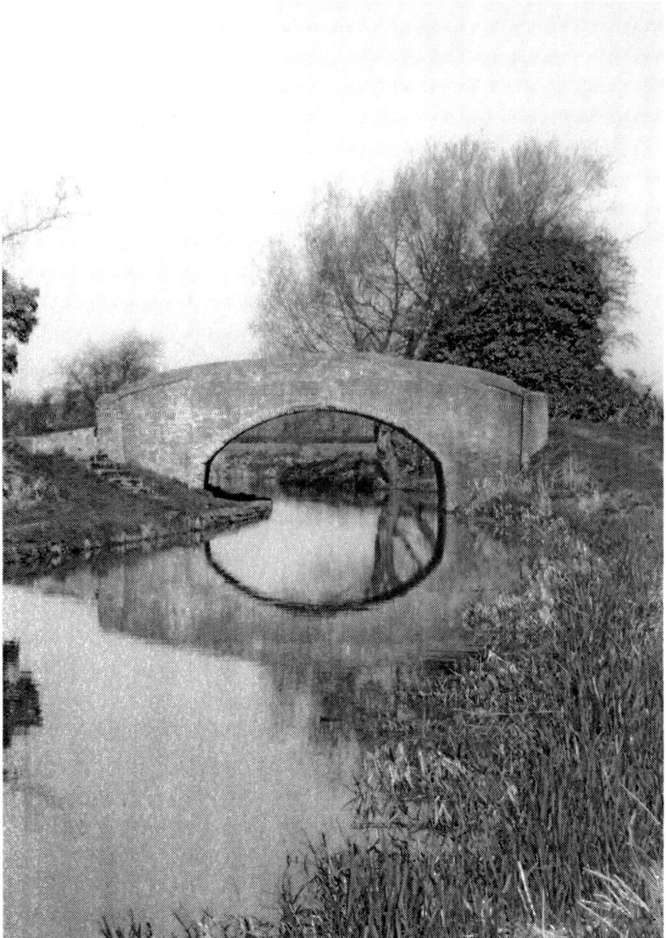

The clock of life is ticking and taking the minutes of your life away.

LOSS

She's dead
The words echoed around
Inside my head.

This is a big issue for me.

A lot has to do with the kind of person you are – your character and personality.

I have always been sentimental and emotional. Sad stuff makes me cry.

There have been many losses in my life such as jobs and marriage but the biggest was the loss of people.

First was the death of my sister. This was the first time I had seen a dead person. I was only thirteen years of age at the time. There was a feeling of unreality. The whole event seemed like a dream. I wish it had been.

I saw and heard the anguish and raw emotion of my parents.

I felt on the outside looking in, a part of what was going on and yet not part.

Two other things that stick in my mind from that time are me playing cards (patience), because it gave me something to do, and the smell of my great aunts. Mothballs! I suppose it was because black clothes were associated with mourning and only came out when there was a death. Nowadays we wear black at any time and don't tend to use mothballs.

My Auntie Doris died next. I liked going to her house because it was linked to fun and laughter.

Auntie Doris was associated with many 'firsts'. She taught me how to ride a bike. She bought me my first grown up petticoat. She gave me my first bible and prayer book, both of which I still have and treasure, just as I treasure her memory.

After this came the death of my maternal grandmother. Throughout my childhood she had always stood by me, supported me, protected me and loved me. I looked forward to her visits. She had a good sense of humour and could reach down to a child's level. I thought my heart would break when she died.

However, little did I know worse was to come.

I know from being a bereavement counsellor and therapist that losing ones parents evokes all kinds of emotions. Losing my parents also released lots of mixed emotions.

As I write this it is sixteen years since my mom died and yet it seems like yesterday – so strong are my memories of that time.

There were times when I was so enveloped by sadness and tears I felt I was drowning in sorrow and no one was able to throw me a life-line. I was awash with anguish. Even to this day I am still affected by her loss.

My grief tore at the very heart of me. I felt like a child, lost and crying for her mother. I hurt so much. There have been some very dark days. There were times when I didn't want to get up and face the day, to look after my family or go to work. Yet I had to. Everything was an effort.

Losing my mom was like losing part of me.

During her life she too had experienced much sadness and unhappiness. Her hurt was my hurt.

I know from my counselling that there are phases of bereavement and sometimes we become stuck in a phase, but I didn't know this at the time.

Becoming a counsellor only happened after the death of my father. I know how important it is to talk about your feelings. However I didn't express my emotions at the time because I felt a nuisance and thought people wouldn't want to hear me going on about how I felt. So I bottled things up.

If you are going through bereavement, please talk to someone about what is going on inside you. This can be friends, family, a willing listener or a professionally trained person.

When I needed something to hold on to
You extended a hand
And led me
Towards life again.
And I was warmed
By your comfort
When cold within,
Knowledge of your caring
Kept me safe.
Words were a guidance
When I had no aim,
And friendship, shelter
To cope with the pain.

Something that helped me was going to see a medium. I found that there were lots of unanswered questions that no one else could answer. The visit resolved many issues.

To anyone reading this who finds themselves in a similar situation, I would say do whatever is right for you. At the time I was discouraged from going because it might make me feel worse. But it didn't. I was glad I went. It was right for me.

My dad's death brought up another issue. From the time I 'failed' the 11+ I had wanted his praise and an acknowledgement of the subsequent successes I gained, but it was not to be. When I sat next to his dead body I knew it was something I would never now receive.

Please don't misunderstand – I loved my dad. This was just the way he was. With his death I didn't have to prove anything to anyone any longer – except myself!

It is important to give yourself praise and approval. This can stop you always looking to others to fulfil your needs.

The stream of time flows on
Taking the years away
Unable to keep them still
They ripple our life away.

Who you are today, isn't who you have to be tomorrow.

UPS AND DOWN, DOWN, DOWNS

This dark abyss is a familiar place
To climb out of again
Deserted strength
Must be regained
To reach the top and remain.

I have had more ups and downs than a ride at the fair. At one time there seemed to be more downs than ups.

Yes I have felt sorry for myself and yes I wallowed in self pity. So, I suppose I felt like a victim. In fact I know I did. Yet now I am a therapist I also know a lot more about being a 'victim'. But logic doesn't come into it.

With victimisation came blame. Boy did I know about blame! Another emotion that goes with blame is anger.

Do I have any magic solutions to give you? No. Solutions take time and effort. Face up to the problems and gradually they will become resolved.

The only way to tackle a problem is to confront it. Ignoring it won't help because like a 'Jack in the box' it keeps on coming up. Neither will hiding from it by drinking alcohol or taking drugs. These may take away the problem for a time but when the influence wears off you are reminded again.

Sooner or later the problem has to be dealt with. By ignoring it the problem grows to insurmountable proportions. Nothing is too big that it can't be sorted out.

If necessary break the problem down into manageable chunks and deal with each of the separate aspects. Putting off dealing with problems only increases the agony.

I have avoided issues and put things off. The reasons being it was easier at the time to avoid confrontation and because I didn't want to stir things up. It felt as if I would awake the sleeping giant.

Sometimes by facing your demons you find they aren't so dreadful after all.

What I will say is it is okay to feel the way you do. You are not silly or stupid. However, do something with what you are experiencing.

Whatever you do don't turn that blame inwards and

say or think things like "I shouldn't ...." or "Why did I .....?".

Write and talk about how you are feeling but don't keep it inside. Holding stuff within keeps you stuck because it isn't going anywhere. Instead it grows and engulfs you and can take you over.

How do I know? I have been there and as the saying goes, 'worn the t-shirt'.

Challenge your beliefs, look at things from every angle and start to maybe change your perceptions. Perceptions can seem like fact when really they aren't real, it is just the way you interpret or represent events.

Perhaps you could even admit, if only to yourself, that you may have been wrong sometimes. Maybe there were things you could have done better. But we are all wise after the event.

If you can – forgive – both yourself and others.

How long does it take to sort things out? I don't know. It takes as long as it takes. You may go two steps forward and one back. At least you are still going forwards. As long as something is happening and you're not stuck.

When I was at a low ebb I had expectations of my family which I thought would make me better. Why didn't they do more? Can't they see I'm not coping?

Eventually I realised the only person that could help me was myself. If you find it hard to pick yourself up then I would recommend seeing a counsellor or therapist. Friends and family can then support you during the process of therapy. You will find more solutions in other sections.

Little by little issues are resolved and life improves.

The hole opened up and I fell in.
Yet it is only now
As I start to climb out,
That I realise –
I had been falling for years.

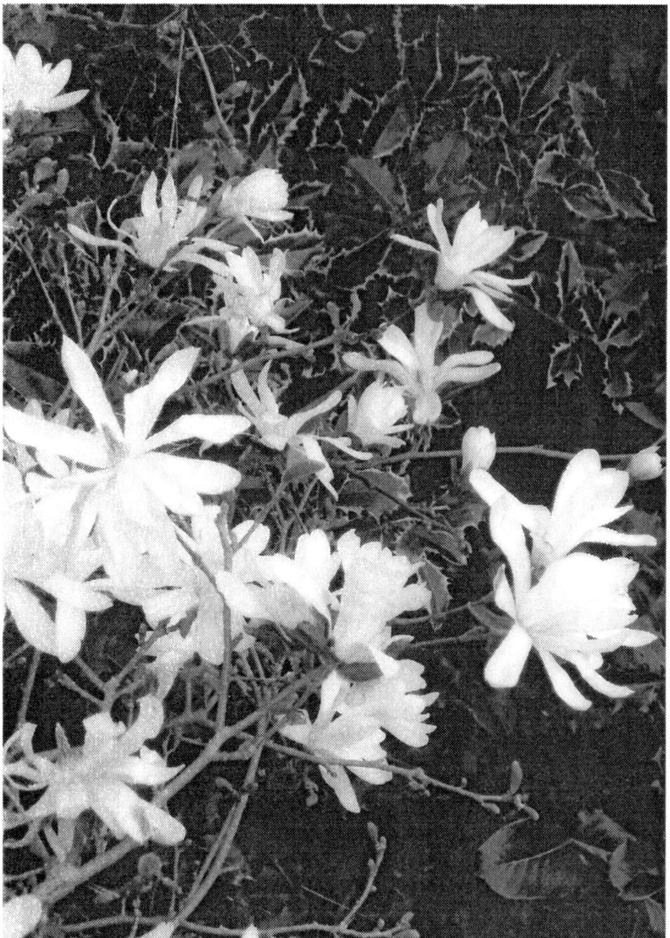

Failure is a stepping stone to success.

FAILURE

*A mirror reflects our image
But the mind reflects our life.*

I didn't fail and I wasn't a failure, but I accepted the title.

When I 'failed' my 11+ I felt branded a failure.

It's only as I look back on my life that I can see my secondary education was a success. I succeeded in many ways but life reminds you of that initial failure and I reinforced the 'not good enough' feeling.

Other people's disappointment became the ball and chain I carried around with me.

At times it seemed I never grew up inside. I was still that eleven year old child who failed.

It is amazing how something like that affects your life.

So it is important to stop the destructive way of thinking and start to be constructive. Change your attitude.

No one fails; we are just learning and sometimes it takes us longer than others. But that's okay as long as we give ourselves permission to learn at our own pace.

Don't be afraid to fail. As a child you failed many times as you tried to walk. But whenever you fell it didn't stop you. You just kept on trying until you succeeded in walking.

One way we support being a failure is through criticism. Are you one of those people that puts yourself down and constantly judges what you do and how you do it?

If so, stop right now.

Think for a minute. Would you say the same statements to anyone else?

No you wouldn't because you don't want to hurt them. Yet you are quite happy to berate and harm yourself. So be kind and look after your feelings the same way you would other people's.

If you look back you will see many accomplishments that have been covered up and hidden by failures. We only see what we want to see.

So look out for those successes. Shake off the dust

of neglect and hold them up. Enjoy looking at these shining examples of your achievements.

> *I looked for success*
> *Without realising*
> *I had it all the time.*

**I sit
I look
I listen
I learn.**

LOOK BEYOND THE PROBLEM

Again I heard the call,
The one I tried to ignore
But find that now I cannot –
No, not any more.
This time there'll be an answer,
Before I hear no more.

It is so easy when problems crop up to become resigned to them. We feel weakened by them, and they seem to engulf us. Sometimes there seems to be no way out. It is as if we are a prisoner to our problems. These feelings can lead to depression.

Yet by adopting an attitude of "what can I do about it", we can look at our options. Having accepted that we can do something we become more empowered. Action is the key that enables us to deal with whatever life throws at us.

The formula is:

Problem – what is the concern?

↓

Aim/goal – what do I want?

↓

Possible solutions – what can I do?

↓

Consequences – what might happen?

↓

Conclusions – what is my decision?

↓

Action/resolution – do it.

↓

Did it work? If not go over the alternatives again.

So find a piece of paper and brainstorm. Ask yourself questions such as the following:
What can I do?
What do I want?
What options do I have?
Who can help me?

This exercise will help you look beyond the problem towards a resolution.

I attended a course once where I had to break a thick piece of wood in half with my hand. The principle of looking beyond the problem applied here. My attention (focus) went past the wood (problem) and so did my hand (implementing action) and therefore going beyond the problem.

Sometimes though we can create problems with the phrase "what if …?"

By asking ourselves this question we are looking past today and projecting into the future which hasn't arrived yet. Because the future is only an illusion as yet we cannot answer our question. As a result we worry until whatever might happen. But events may not happen.

However the anticipation and distress caused by a vivid imagination can be worse that the event itself.

Do we worry about what might happen if we run out of bread or milk next week or next month? No, of course we don't because we know that we will just go out and buy more. In the same way we also know that whatever problems have cropped up, we usually solve them.

A technique I use when I find myself creating negative pictures and scenes is to stop the action, rewind the film and cancel. Basically I am adopting the function of a video or DVD recorder. Other times when I am having negative dialogues I tell myself to 'shut up'!

*The way opens up
I begin to see clearly.*

Invest in yourself, by spending time and effort on you.

MAKING CHANGES

I change my clothes
I change my hair
Changes go on everywhere.

Changes are those little tweaks we give to our life which can break habits and improve the quality of our existence.

It's good to change what doesn't work.

Some changes are inevitable and necessary and sometimes brought about without choice. Change is a natural part of life.

But what stops us from making these changes? It can be:

Fear of the unknown
Fear of failure
What other people may think
It feels safer not to try
Making the wrong choice.

Until we make the change how do we know what will be the result? To know that something needs changing means dissatisfaction with the present format.

To make a change we need to feel good about ourselves. Confidence and self esteem come in useful here to believe in what we are doing and to know that any improvement is better than what is going on at present.

- Maybe you want to change habits such as smoking, eating, drinking too much alcohol and adopt a healthier attitude to life.

- Maybe you want to feel happier and so eliminate or alter the things that you know pull you down.

- Maybe you want to achieve personal growth by changing your job or taking a course.

- Maybe you want to overcome fears and be more confident and outgoing.

Whatever the changes may be I want you to know that you have the ability to make them.

Communication is important. The words we and others use can be tools or weapons. Sometimes what others say can be open to misinterpretation. Are we really listening or at times only picking up certain words or phrases? Are you so used to hearing criticism that, that is all you expect to hear?

Start changing the words you use in association with yourself. Don't put yourself down. Use words and phrases that will enable you to achieve the changes you envisage for yourself.

If you want to make changes to your life then you have to make decisions based on what it is you want to alter, or maybe make some new choices.

There will always be obstacles but keep going.

Research shows that people are successful when they set themselves goals.

Keep thinking about what you want – what you desire and make those changes happen.

Is this really me?
Where has she gone?
That person from yesteryear.
So much has changed
Yet there is still work to be done.

You are what you think – so make your thoughts count.

CONFIDENCE

*I boldly go where
I haven't been before.*

Confidence and self esteem can both be depleted as a result of:

How little praise and encouragement we receive
What people tell us
What we come to believe
How we are treated
Not living up to expectations (yours and other people's)
Being put down (by yourself and others)
Trying and failing
Other people's attitudes and reactions
Illness
What was said to you as a child
Changes you've made that made things worse
Being unsure of what you really want
The way we cope with life.

So what is confidence?

It can be many things including having faith in your talents and abilities. Trusting in yourself and believing in what you can do. It is taking a risk and moving out of your comfort zone.

What words define confidence?

Strength	courage	capability
Self-assurance	boldness	dependence
Faith	empowerment	self-reliance
Trust	self-belief	daring

Where does confidence come from?

Ourselves
Our environment
Other people
We act it out

What you tell yourself does affect what you do. When you tell yourself you can't then you won't. So even if it is difficult tell yourself you can do whatever it is you want to achieve. The mind is very powerful and so are your thoughts. Use this power as a turbo boost to propel yourself forward.

Having confidence is being able to step out of your comfort zone into a state of discomfort. By doing this regularly the uncomfortable becomes comfortable.
I remember the first time I gave a talk to a group of people. I was terrified. Now because of how many I have given I am more at ease.

There are lots of things you are confident about doing. These can be at home, at work or in social situations. However you overlook them and don't see them as demonstrations of confidence. Someone else may look at you and believe you are confident.

Look back at what you once found difficult but which you now find easy.

> *Armed with self belief*
> *And a bag of courage*
> *I emerge from beneath*
> *My doubts and fears*
> *To take on the world.*

Love is not only words but actions.

DIVORCE

*I am lost
And need to be found.
Where am I?
Am I still around?*

They say the only winners in divorce are the solicitors. At least solicitors can walk away from the situation.

The guilt, blame, resentment, anger and acrimony lasted a long time after the solicitors had received their fee.

Divorce throws up a lot of emotional balls and it is impossible to juggle them without dropping some.

Somehow, although the file is closed, the events are still open. It is like a cut that doesn't heal and every now and then the scab is knocked off and it bleeds.

My present husband and I met whilst going through

our respective divorces. His was more bitter than my own but because we were together I also experienced some of the impact. Believe me I really did feel the force.

(I must hasten to add that this isn't the case for everyone, but I am writing about my own experience.)

Yes the hurts do lessen but the baggage accumulated during the process is difficult to get rid of.

There were times when I thought I was going to burst, so intense were the feelings and emotions.

I have worked hard on resolving these and many other problems and difficulties so that the final season of my life can be peaceful and harmonious.

The beginning of any new relationship is full of excitement and expectation as each person explores the infinite possibilities of the budding romance. At the time life takes on a new meaning.

For me the paint was hardly dry on the hearts and flowers when the problems started and reality kicked in.

Looking back I can see that there is never a right or wrong way of doing things. There is only what you did at the time with the information and experience available.

Someone once said there ought to be a degree in

retrospection and I know what they mean. It is only when you look back that you see how things could have been different. However, at the time you are driven by emotions and intense feelings that are fuelled by what is going on at the time.

Back then it was like being in a war zone.

Yet despite all odds we are still together. Our relationship was sorely tested and at times it seemed easier to get out than to stay in. But stay in I did.

The sunshine has come
To warm my heart
The chill of neglect departs
There's a fire within
What feelings it imparts.
I cannot know what lies ahead
Perhaps it's wisest not
For I want this ray of light
To shatter the dark of night.

We learn from our mistakes, but when the lesson is over – let go.

ANGER

*The anger ripped through me
And tore me apart.*

Anger can come out of nowhere. A sudden thought or memory can unleash strong reactions. Events from the past that haven't been resolved suddenly open up.

Anger is like a volcano erupting. It is fired by passion and rage.

Feel the anger. What is it telling you? What are you avoiding? Who's upsetting you? What aren't you dealing with? Is someone pressing your buttons? Are you angry with yourself?

My anger came from wishing I had been more assertive, from frustrations and past injustices.

My ego kept bringing them up and reminding me. That's what the ego does. It's like having a wicked little gremlin on your shoulder that talks in your ear bringing up the troublesome past and worries you about the fearful future. As the ego lives in the past and future it does not inhabit the present, so stay mindful and you avoid the menace.

Remember the ego cannot survive without judgement.

Some of my anger wasn't with other people, it was really with me. I may have blamed them. By reacting to other people's behaviour I was giving away my power. As we need our personal power, we can't afford to give any away.

So take control and admit any responsibility which is yours. Any past issues can be looked at in terms of how they affect you in the present.

Anger is a feeling and emotionally charged. Do you need to feel this way?

If you are the cause, stop blaming and start forgiving. In ten or twenty years' time it won't have the same impact or importance and in fact you may not even remember the event. Put things in proportion to the rest of your life.

Powerful waves
Incessant and strong
Red hot feelings
Surging emotions
Rise and engulf
What was once tranquil and calm.

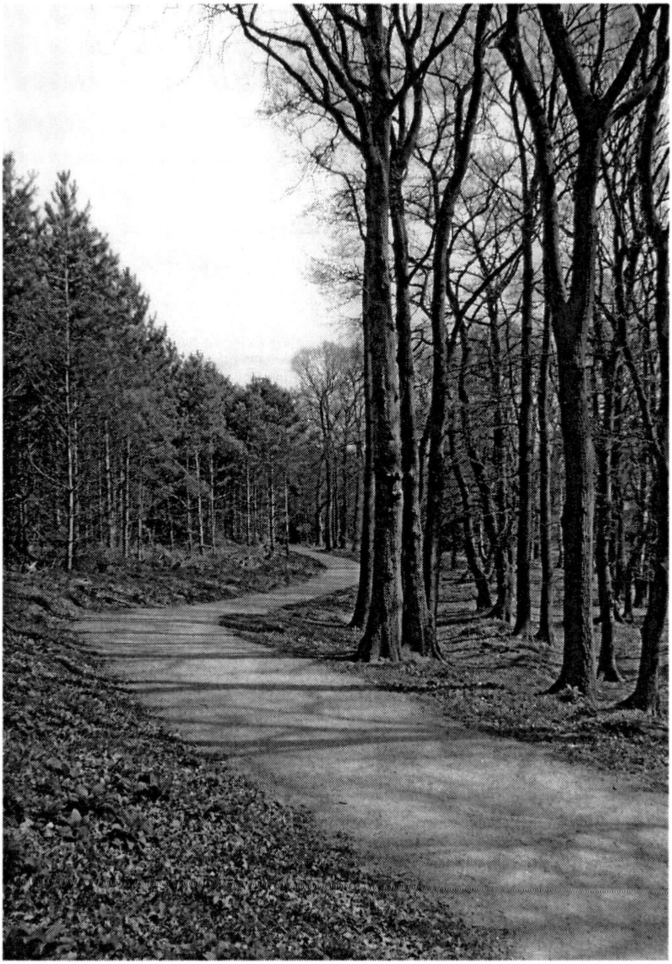

You are important – so be kind to yourself.

CRITICISM

Words are wounds that scar me

I have beaten myself up so badly with harsh words and negative thoughts. It was a kind of self-flagellation.

Did I deserve it? I thought so at the time.

Because I had lived with criticism I always tried to do everything right. Unfortunately life does not necessarily conspire to help. Looking back I didn't know any better. When you know better you can do better.

Other people's criticism has left me battered and bruised. Their words destroyed my confidence and I felt vulnerable. Sometimes I would be sad and hurt and at other times I would be angry and vengeful.

I could do nothing about the words of others but my own I could. What other people say, do or think is their responsibility. What I say, do or think is my responsibility.

In the same way what you say, do or think is your responsibility.

Remember you can't change other people, only they can change themselves, if they want to. However you can change yourself by what you say.

Words can either be creative or destructive. They are either tools or weapons. Think about how you use words. Choose words that pick you up rather than dash you down.

Don't accept criticism from other people without checking it out first and asking yourself if it is true. If it isn't 'bin it' or if it is, ask 'what am I going to do about such a negative appraisal'?

Not by chance do words such as self-esteem, self confidence, self worth, and self approval start with the words 'self'.

I have looked outside myself for approval and have suffered from the 'disease to please'. Criticism has picked away at my self-esteem. Now I know that approval comes from the inside. We have to approve of ourselves. When we look to other people for their approval it is a sign that we are not giving it to ourselves.

I know it is difficult to change habits, because I am still trying to change some of mine. However, it is possible. With time and perseverance you can work wonders.

DO IT FOR YOU, BECAUSE YOU ARE WORTH IT.

I want you to remember three important words:

PRAISE   SUPPORT   ENCOURAGEMENT

Start to praise yourself. Acknowledge the things that go well. Even the smallest achievement needs to be recognised. If you have only ever used criticism then this will be difficult to start with.

With any bad habit it is better to replace it with a good one. So awareness is the key. Be supportive and give yourself a lot of encouragement. Be your own best friend.

Learn to say 'well done' more and give yourself a pat on the back often.

During periods of change you will go through a time of discomfort. This is normal. Keep supporting yourself with kind words and if you do lapse into criticism then replace the words or thoughts with something encouraging. Keep telling yourself how well you are doing. Look back occasionally to see just how far you have come.

So start by building your 'self' up and re-defining your image. But remember a positive mental image needs maintaining so do not stop. If you do lapse bring in lots of reinforcement. Be generous.

From adversity springs growth.

When you find your voice
You have a choice.

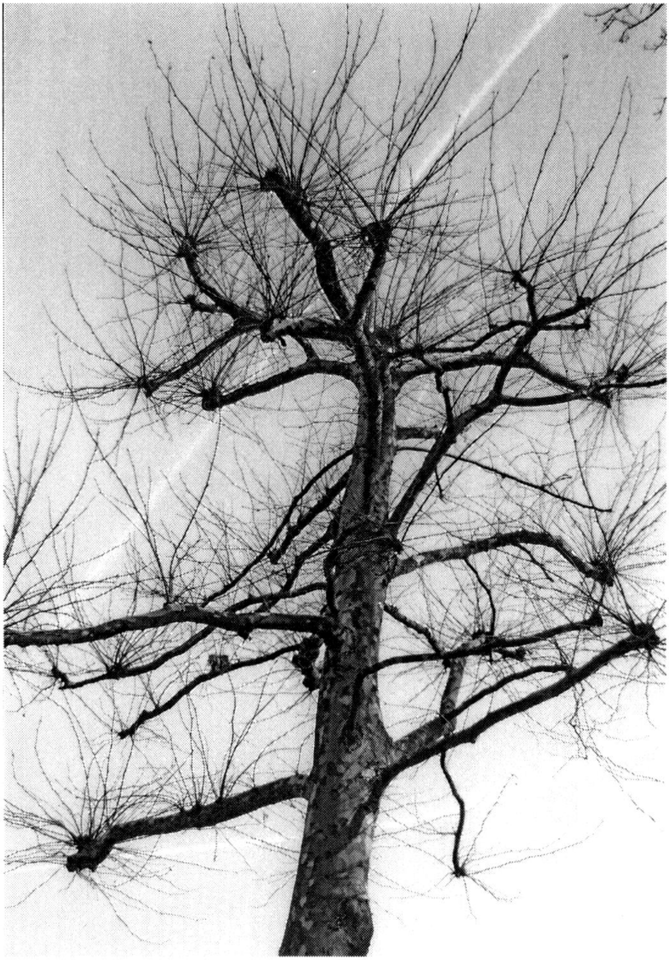

Words are powerful – so use them wisely.

FORGIVENESS

My heart has been hurt
My pride damaged
The past holds pain
And plenty of baggage.

This is a difficult subject to write about. It also exposes the 'practise what you preach' philosophy.

Time is a healer because I can look upon some of the slights and injustices of the past without being affected in the same way. So the key may be to wait until the event or situation has faded enough not to arouse the old grievances and emotions. Then you, like myself, may find it easier to forgive and let go the past.

Obviously in order to forgive, some transgression had to have taken place initially. You will also find that some instances are easier to forgive than others.

Emotions that I have felt include hurt, anger, sadness, resentment, and, I hate to admit, revenge. A sense of wanting to avenge the wounds inflicted and the emotional upheaval caused.

There are people I have forgiven but there are others that at the moment I find it difficult to forgive.

Logically I know that by holding on to the resentment I also hold on to the people and the event or situation, but at the moment the wounds are too deep, and hurt too much.

You will know when the time is right to forgive. Other people, events and situations may have come along since that reduce the impact and so the significance may not be as strong. Even the forgiving does not mean that you have to like the person or to condone their behaviour. It just means letting them and what they did go.

Sometimes though, when you keep on revisiting a memory it can take on more importance and significance. The result can be something which has grown out of proportion. So strip it back to its original size.

Throughout life people will throw all kinds of statements your way. The trick is not to catch them. Don't accept anything unless you agree. Question the integrity of the comments. Are they true?

The small stuff is easier to deal with. So don't hang on to these minor minnows. You and your inner spirit are more important. So cleanse yourself often and get rid of the clutter. Free yourself from the debris of doubt.

The big stuff is harder to deal with. As I said earlier, time is a great healer as it smoothes things down and when you look back the size and impact isn't the same. The emotions don't hit you in quite the same way.

You will know when the time is right to forgive and let go.

Importantly, remember to also forgive yourself.

I forgive
And let go,
Bitter memories
And many a foe.
I reclaim my life
And on I go.

Remember that you are good enough – so believe it.

BELIEFS

*Beliefs are the roots
From which we grow.*

Beliefs are important. Beliefs are the roots from which your life grows.

A belief is an idea you hold true about yourself, your life, your image, your environment and other people. It is an underlying assumption like a construction.

Negative beliefs are just like children's building blocks – they can be knocked down or changed.

Limiting beliefs can keep us stuck thereby preventing us from moving on and achieving. Our beliefs influence our thoughts, and these thoughts influence how we behave.

Behaviour can be kept in place by fears, payoffs and hidden agendas. By stopping the unwanted behaviour, your habits can change and also your attitudes.

Our relationships with other people can be affected especially if we compare ourselves to them. Our opinions and imagination can be false friends. So stop your imagination running amok because you may react as if it is real. Take a reality check and ask yourself if what you believe is really true.

Put things in proportion if you tend to exaggerate. Yes it might feel as if your whole life is permeated by problems, but is it really?

Thoughts support and maintain the beliefs either we, or someone else, has created. These ideas are programmed into us and affect our daily lives.

I know that the wrong beliefs can lower confidence and self esteem. So it is important to look at these beliefs to see if they are working for you or against you. Beliefs can be changed.

So ask yourself, what beliefs do you want?

For example, suppose you want to lose weight. At the moment you may be saying, "I can't lose weight", and this isn't inspiring or motivating. If you change this statement to, "I am losing weight", and then combine this phrase with imagining yourself slimmer; wow, what a powerful team.

In this respect imagination can work for you. So use your imagination to create what you want and not what you don't want.

What stops us from making changes? This can be

fear of the unknown, fear of failure, what other people think, making the wrong choice and sometimes it can feel safer not to try.

> *I believe I can*
> *I believe I am*
> *I believe I will.*

Put the sunshine into your life and smile.

MAKE THE MOST OF LIFE

The sands of time
Are running out
And grains of age
Accumulate.

I remember when my children were born people said make the most of them now because they soon grow up. They were right.

Now as I am in the autumn of my life I can look back and think how quickly time has passed. Where have all those years gone?

People are now saying to me to make the most of every day because you never know what's going to happen! It sounds like either a threat or a warning. What is worse, I even find myself saying the same phrase.

So just lately I have been giving life and its meaning a lot of thought. How do we make the most of every day?

For me it is not doing so much housework, because housework can wait whereas I can't. Instead I take time out for me to do the things I prefer to do.

Think and talk in terms of 'wanting to' rather than 'having to'. The latter statement sounds compulsory whereas the former gives the impression of desire. So choose what you want to do rather than feeling obliged because you 'should', 'ought', or 'must'.

So what can you do to make the most of your life?

Look at what you enjoy doing and fit more of these pleasures into each day. Make more time for yourself and challenge the chores you do automatically. Stop feeling guilty about whatever you put to one side.

Be honest with yourself. This is your life. Give yourself choice and do whatever it is that brings you fulfilment, happiness and contentment.

Don't let age be a barrier. If there is something you want to do – do it. If you have the enthusiasm and determination then have a go. Never look back with regret and wish you had.

The things I did later in life were to study for a new career, karate chop a thick piece of wood in half, go white water rafting, abseil and do a fire walk.

Also remember to stop all the 'doing' and relax. Take time to chill out, read or simply look around you.

Why are we always rushing?
Where are we going to?
Hurrying our lives away
We're hardly ever still.
Perhaps we ought to stop
And check where we're travelling to.

Every now and then it's good to come off the motorway of life and draw into a lay-by.

LOOKING TO THE FUTURE

*When you make things happen in your mind
You can make them happen in your life.*

None of us can know what the future holds, however we can have some influence.

How do you want your life to be? What happens in the present can have a great bearing on the future.

I have always wanted to be artistic but discounted my talent. Comparing myself to others didn't help. However I now know that I can develop my own talents and abilities.

How often have you compared yourself?

How often have you said, 'I can't'? Can't is a dead end street that is taking you nowhere.

My children could never tell which was a horse, cow or dog when I drew for them. It seems my skills haven't improved by the look my grandson gave me when I told him the pictures I had drawn were of him and his mom and dad. He stared at the drawings really hard but didn't appear to find a resemblance!

I want to do more painting. A Constable I am not but I love mixing colours together to form a painting. Some people might dispute the term 'painting' but it is to me and that's what matters. It is all relative and it gives me a great deal of pleasure.

So with the future in mind I have bought myself a couple of canvases. I haven't painted on canvas before so it will be with trepidation that I put brush to cloth. I have painted the covers to some of my CDs but a canvas is bigger and a great deal more daunting.

However with some of my own good advice and encouragement I shall be having a go.

Self-talk can either be a hazard or a help. So be your own best friend. I know that I shall be giving myself a great deal of enjoyment by sitting and dabbling.

So express yourself through what you do. Start now and write a list of what you want to experiment with. Too many of us are put off by listening to other people's negativity as well as our own.

Meanwhile the clock of life is ticking, taking the minutes of your life away.

We hold the future in every thought and decision we make.

You are your own best friend.

CONCLUSION

*Each day is your great gift
So use it well.*

In writing this book I hope it will help the reader to know that they are not alone in experiencing highly emotive states and strong feelings.

Despite all my family and friends there were times when I felt very alone with how I felt.

Reliving some of the events was difficult, painful and emotional, but if writing this book brings hope and inspiration to you the reader then I am happy.

So believe in yourself, who you are and what you want. Search for the truth and don't live a lie. By changing yourself you may influence other people and as a result they may change themselves.

You are special and your life is important. So start today to create the future you want for yourself.

Remember also that achieving your goals isn't half as important as the person you become in setting and pursuing them.

I wish my readers all I would wish for myself.

As I walk
Through the avenues of life,
There is time to reflect,
And see the panorama of years past.

Memories that flit across one's vision;
Filtering files
Of cloud and sunshine,
Clear skies and rain.

Stiles of trouble
Are mounted and overcome.
Fields of happiness,
Spread out in the sun.

The scenery ever changing,
The seasons that arrive and depart,
They help make up a story,
Of which life is the heart.

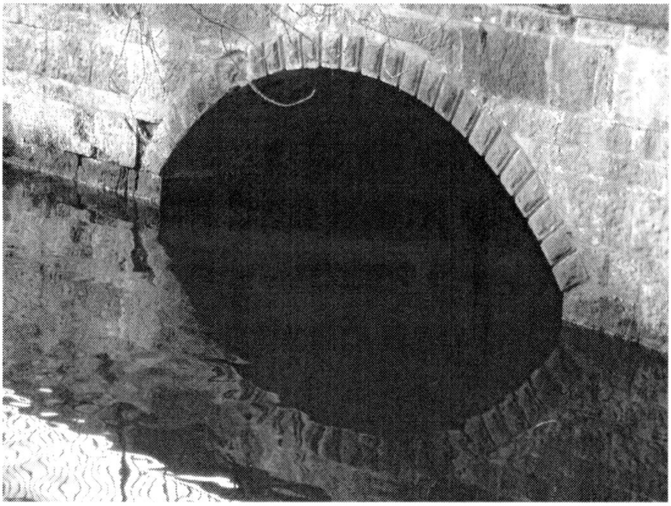

I am free
No longer controlled
By anyone
But me
I am free.

I can change
I'm in charge
My mind and life
I'll rearrange
I can change.

I believe in me
So I can be
Whoever and
Whatever I want to be
Because
I believe in me.

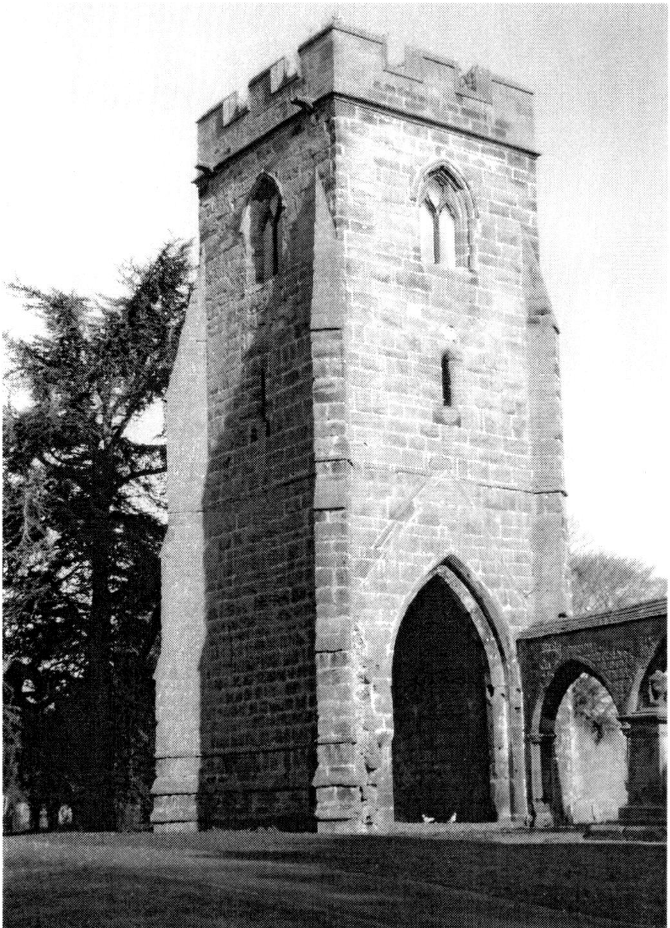

PEACE, PERFECT PEACE

I find myself in silence
Time becomes a balm
To smooth out all the wrinkles
And produce a state of calm.

CDs available by the same Author:

Time for You
Helps you to unwind and relieve tension and anxiety. Giving time to you sends powerful and positive internal messages that enhances well-being and self esteem.

To Help you Sleep
Sleep is a natural remedy against stress. This CD will help you relax and sleep at bedtime or any other time.

Relieve your Irritable Bowel Syndrome
Written specifically for IBS sufferers. Research shows that relaxation has a very positive effect on IBS and in some cases actually relieves the symptoms and aids recovery. This is especially so in the case of stress IBS.

Support for the Difficult Times in Life
There are times in life that challenge us. Relaxation can give you the strength and clarity needed during these difficult times. This CD will enable you to feel stronger and more supported. This is a beautiful recording and can also be used as a guided meditation with tree images and secret garden.

Relaxation Therapy
This CD will help you to relax both mentally and

physically. Life can be very demanding and the accompanying tension can lead to many stress-related illnesses, so it is important to relax. You will benefit every time you listen to this CD.

Be a Success
Turbo charge your motivation and kick start your confidence, determination and will to succeed. Become inspired so your dreams become a reality.

For more information and details on how you can order these and other products go to www.janicejohnson.co.uk

About the Author

Having made the decision to make a complete career change, Janice, studied for an Open University honours degree in Psychology whilst looking after her family, a home and working full time. In addition she also gained professional qualifications in hypnotherapy and psychotherapy, later adding counselling and life coaching. Having herself suffered the loss of close family she became a volunteer bereavement counsellor to help others to cope with, and share their grief.

Having made life changing decisions herself, she has enjoyed helping others to improve their lives. She knows that to make any change is a hard decision and even more difficult to put it into action. It is so easy to put things off. However, the benefits of making these changes far outweigh the effort.

Her work is fascinating, fulfilling and rewarding and in the process she has met some amazing and wonderful people.